Women
in the
Ministry

Bridget Steib

WOMEN IN THE MINISTRY by Bridget Steib

Published by Christian Living Books
4451 Parliament Place
Lanham, MD 20706
www.pneumalife.com

Unless otherwise noted, all Scripture quotations are from the Holy Bible, New International Version. Copyright © 1973, 1978, 1984, International Bible Society. Used by permission.

Scripture quotations marked NKJV are from the New King James Version of the Bible. Copyright © 1979, 1980, 1982 by Thomas Nelson, Inc., publishers. Used by permission.

Scripture quotations marked KJV are from the King James Version of the Bible.

Copyright © 2001 by Bridget Steib
All rights reserved
International Standard Book Number: 1-5622-171-8
March 2001, first printing

Printed in the United States of America

a division of Pneuma Life Publishing

Dedication

This book is dedicated to my loving husband, Joseph P. Steib, Sr., who is such an encouragement and inspiration. And to my three children—Shondra, Joseph, Jr., and Princess.

Ellen Barnes, who is my loving, sweet, precious mother and my biological brothers and sisters.

Also to the entire Ministry of Love family.

Acknowledgements

I would like to acknowledge Evangelist Ora Bradford, who is not only my sister in Christ, but also my biological sister. As the assistant pastor of the Ministry of Love, she works so diligently and faithfully along with my husband and I. She is an inspiration, strength, and support to me. We work together as a team to see the work of God in the ministry carried out.

I am truly indebted to Bernetta Knighten, my personal secretary, who deserves special recognition. She has been my "leaning post" in all avenues of this project.

Special gratitude goes to Mrs. Rose Carter, Mrs. Shirley Singleton, Mrs. Dianne Williams, and Mrs. Pearl Matthews, who have been a tremendous help in getting this book together.

Most of all, I acknowledge the Holy Trinity.

Table of Contents

Foreword

When I first heard the message preached, *"Women in the Ministry,"* it set me free! And I know many men and women will be set free, too!

This book is based upon Pastor Steib's experience as a woman in the ministry. As a wife, a mother, and a pastor, she can share some vital information with you. Knowing the challenges that she endured by answering the call of God on her life; her priorities are God first, family second, and church third: a woman of faith!

I thank God for giving Pastor Steib revelation knowledge of the scriptures. As she teaches, knowledge is power, and it will cause you to dominate.

I give all my blessings to my sister, my pastor, one of the greatest persons I know. She has been and still is a blessing to me, and I know she will be a blessing to you. Truly a pastor and teacher after God's own heart, she feeds her sheep with knowledge and understanding.

Having known Pastor Steib all my life, I feel privileged to say that this book will certainly answer many questions regarding women in the ministry. This book will allow men and women the opportunity to know their purpose in the ministry and to understand the spirit world.

My sister is number one, and you will surely be blessed!

I have watched you grow from a child to a mature woman in the Lord. I salute you, Pastor Bridget Steib. You are one of the greatest.

—EVANGELIST ORA BRADFORD, ASSISTANT PASTOR
THE MINISTRY OF LOVE

"Except the Lord build the house, they labour in vain that build it: except the Lord keep the city, the watchman waketh but in vain."

—PSALM 127:1

Chapter 1

Establishing Your Foundation in Ministry

Many well-meaning believers in the church today look at ministry as if it is natural, but it's not. Ministry is supernatural. We simply have to believe God and have faith for everything. We have to believe Him for the people, finances, and so forth. Faith says it is already done. To believe is to accept it as real and true. So have faith that it is done and believe that it is already given, no matter what the problem is or what the need may be!

God did not call us to figure Him out; God says to only believe Him. He did not tell us to perform any miracles. He tells us to simply speak His Word and He will perform the miracles. (See Jeremiah 1:9, 12.)

Learn not to build your church or ministry on visions, dreams or prophecies. Make sure everything is built on the Word of God. Be careful and always make the Word of God your foundation for everything. God's Word tells us in Psalm 127:1: "Except the Lord build the house, they labour in vain that build it: except the Lord keep the city, the watchman waketh but in vain."

Jesus said in Matthew 16:18, "Upon this rock I build my church and the gates of hell shall not prevail..." The rock is Jesus; He is the Word of God. The church is the believer. Believers are to be built on the Word of God. Make sure you have the Word of God rooted in your heart so when the winds blow and the rains fall, you will not be moved. If God establishes your ministry, not a weapon in hell can prevail against it. Realize you are not operating in your own strength, but by the divine ability of God.

Here is wisdom concerning ministry. After witnessing miracles performed by Jesus, Nicodemus observed, "No man could do this except God be with him" (John 3:2). In Acts 5:39, a Pharisee by the name of Gamaliel said, "But if it is of God, you cannot overthrow it least you even be found to fight against God." And in Romans 8:31, Paul tell us, "If God is for us, who can be against us?"

"He will also go before Him in the spirit and power of Elijah, to turn the hearts of the fathers to the children, and the disobedient to the wisdom of the just, to make ready a people prepared for the Lord."

—LUKE 1:17

Chapter 2

Jesus and His Cousin

Let's look at Jesus and His cousin, John the Baptist. The Bible says in Luke 1:36 that the angel of the Lord spoke to Mary and said, "And, behold, thy cousin Elisabeth, she hath also conceived a son in her old age: and this is the sixth month with her, who was called barren."

Jesus and John the Baptist were born six months apart—John was six months older than Jesus. Jesus and John grew up together, emotionally and spiritually speaking. But John still did not know his cousin was the Messiah, even after growing up together. I can imagine how they walked, talked, and played with each other during their childhood, and how they probably stayed with one another.

Still John did not know that his own cousin was the Christ. Jesus must have demonstrated such spirit of humility. He had to be "some kind of humble" to walk with his cousin for the first 30 years of His life and yet never reveal He was the Messiah.

Isn't it amazing how people can be around you all the time, yet they do not know you? Paul said, "For what man knoweth the things of a man, save the spirit of man which is in him? Even so the things of God knoweth no man, but the Spirit of God" (1 Cor. 2:11). In other words, nobody knows you like you—and God. And, no one knows you unless the Holy Spirit reveals you to them. John the Baptist did not know Jesus because the Spirit had not yet revealed to him that his cousin was the Messiah.

Scripture also says: "And I knew him not: but he that sent me to baptize with water, the same said unto me, Upon whom thou shalt see the Spirit descending, and remaining on him, the same is he which baptizeth with the Holy Ghost" (John 1:33). You would think from reading just this verse that it was the first time John had ever seen Jesus. Yet they had known each other since infancy.

What John the Baptist is actually saying is that he did not *know* Jesus in the spirit. For thirty years he knew Jesus in the natural, but he did not know Jesus in the spirit. Many people really do not know you except when God reveals you to them.

John the Baptist knew Jesus was the Messiah when the anointing was upon him. When the anointing lifted, he asked if Jesus was the true Messiah or should they look for another. (See Matthew 11:3.)

You know when you are on a "Holy Ghost high." You have the faith to know, but when the anointing lifts, you have a tendency to feel that you do not know anymore. That's why God deals with the heart of a person (their spirit), so they can know and not just feel. God did not tell you to *feel* something—He said to *know*.

John the Baptist said that he must decrease and Jesus must increase. Many people could not accept Jesus as the Messiah, all because John did not realize that he himself had come as the spiritual Elijah. Jesus, at that time, could not increase because many people were pointing to John, who should've had the people pointing to Jesus.

The people thought John was the Messiah: "And they asked him, saying, Why then do you baptize if you are not the Christ, nor Elijah, nor the Prophet?." (John 1:25).

Luke 1:13 says, "Elisabeth was to have a son and his name was to be called John." Luke 1:17 says, "He would also go before Jesus in the spirit and power of Elijah to turn the hearts of the fathers to the children, and the disobedient to the wisdom of the just; to make ready a people prepared for the Lord."

The Jewish people had knowledge of God's Word. They knew it was prophesied that Elijah was to come before the Messiah. All because John the Baptist did not recognize that he was the "Elijah to come." Many people could not accept Jesus as the Messiah.

In Malachi 3:5 it was prophesied that Elijah the prophet would be sent before the coming of the great and dreadful day of the Lord and He would turn the hearts of the fathers to the children and the hearts of the children to their fathers. Malachi was speaking of what was to take place after the rapture of the church. The true man Elijah would come before the second advent of Jesus Christ.

So John the Baptist, according to Luke 1:17, came in the spirit of Elijah. But this is the testimony of John that sadly came to be: When the Jews sent priests and Levites to ask him, "Who are you?", he did not deny but confessed, "I am not the Christ." They then asked him, "What then? Are you Elijah?" He answered, "I am not." "Are you the prophet?" they asked. He answered, "No" (John 1:19).

In Matthew 17:10-13, you can see how confusion started because Jesus was saying Elijah had already come and John was saying he was not the Elijah. His disciples asked Jesus: "Why then say the scribes that Elijah must first come?" Jesus answered: "...I say unto you, that Elijah is come already, and they knew him not, but have done unto him whatsoever they wished. Likewise shall also the Son of man suffer of them. Then the disciples understood that he spake unto them of John the Baptist."

It is very important to know who you are and what your purpose is. Stop trying to prove or persuade people of who you are or what's your calling and purpose. Be like Jesus—He didn't try to convince anyone as to whom He was because He knew and that was the most important thing.

Jesus was never angry or envious of John the Baptist for having started his ministry before Him. Jesus had confidence knowing who He was and knowing that right time time would come for His ministry to be revealed.

As ministers, it is very important for us to have patience. Hebrews 6:15 tells us, "And so, after he had patiently endured, he obtained the promise."

When you discover your calling or purpose, remember to put your all into it. Give it all you've got! Put your time and your entire heart and soul in it. One way of recognizing your calling is to be aware of the deep desire in your spirit. Remember, God deals with the spirit of our being; God contacts and relates only to our spirit. The desire He puts in your spirit becomes your desire. God wants His desire to become your desire so that He can fulfill His purpose in your life.

"But made himself of no reputation, and took upon him
the form of a servant, and was made in the likeness of men."

—PHILIPPIANS 2:7

Chapter 3

The Subtle Messiah— Jesus and His Family

Just imagine it: Jesus walking, talking, playing, working with His family and friends for thirty-three-and-a-half long years—all the while His family not knowing who He was. They did not know they were living with the Messiah, the covenant-maker and the lawgiver. Matthew 13:55-56 says Jesus had brothers and sisters. No one knew they were living and walking with the Messiah.

Even today, we never know who we're really sitting next to or working with or talking to. That's why it is very important to let God's love in you be spread abroad by the Holy Ghost and to know how to treat everybody. Be aware of how you treat a stranger—they just might be an angel! That same person you did not want to sit by or talk to could be your next president or your next worldwide evangelist. They could be the person God is raising up to be a blessing, not only to you, but to the world.

Jesus never tried to convince anyone that He was the Messiah. Likewise, there is only one person who needs convincing of your calling and that's you! You're the only one who needs to know—not other people. Stop trying to convince, prove, or persuade others. If you are looking for people to approve of you, you'll eventually end up disapproved—and disappointed. Why? Because people will always see a fault.

There were so many faults and criticisms presented about Jesus that He was not accepted by many. Some said He could not be the Messiah because He was just a carpenter's son. Others said He did not go to their schools. The least in the eyes of man is always great in the eyes of God. Man found so many different faults as to why Jesus could not be the Messiah until they could not see God. But Jesus knew it was not for them to know His purpose. It was for Him and Him alone to know because only He could fulfill the promise.

Paul spoke of Christ's humbleness in Philippians 2:7, "But made himself of no reputation, and took upon him the form of a servant, and was made in the likeness of men." When a person abases himself, God will exalt him. Jesus was exalted so high that, according to Paul, "God also hath highly exalted him, and given Him a name which is above every name" (Phil. 2:9).

It is good to have self-confidence, but always remember to remain humble so God can exalt you in your ministry, business or community. You don't have to go around saying who you are, your gift will make room for you.

Notice how Jesus did not want any recognition for Himself. In John 7, His brother wanted Him to be seen of men. Never do anything to be seen of people—just know God sees you. To do things to be seen of men is called flesh glory. That is when man is getting the glory and not God. Jesus always pleased the Father. His will was to do the Father's will and to bring glory to God here on earth.

Jesus had to have been quite humble not to have revealed that He was the Messiah during all those growing-up years. Even His own brothers and sisters did not know Him. Yet, He never stopped for a moment to soothe their curiosity. I can imagine all the teaching and preaching that Jesus did. It may have seemed as if He was not even being heard. But guess what? Even for us, people are listening and watching all the time.

It would appear that Jesus' brothers never heard a word He said, but according to Paul, James believed after Christ was resurrected that He was the Messiah (1 Cor. 15:7). James wrote much of what Jesus said and writes in his epistle that he felt unworthy being called the Lord's brother because of his doubt and disbelief that Jesus was the Messiah. Instead, James acknowledged himself as a servant of the Lord.

Keep doing what God has told you to do. Keep building what God has called you to build. God will place you in certain positions and situations so that something can be proven—not to Him—but to you.

I hear people saying, "I'm going to prove to God that I can stand no matter what." Or, "I'll prove to God that I'm going to preach, sing or whatever the case may be." God then allows them to get in awkward positions, not for something to be proven to Him, but for something to be proven to them.

God is omnipresent (all-present), omnipotent (all-powerful), and omniscient (all-knowing). He knows all things! He already knows if you'll stand! But do you know if you will?

In 1 Kings 19:19-21, the Bible talks about the call of Elisha. Even though Elijah knew Elisha was going to be the next prophet, he wanted Elisha to come to this realization himself. One day Elijah passed by Elisha and threw his mantle on him. Elisha left the oxen, ran after Elijah and said, "Please let me kiss my father and mother, and then I will follow you."

Elijah knew Elisha was going to be the prophet who takes his place, but he wanted Elisha to know. So he told him, "Go back again, for what have I done to you." Notice how Elijah first threw the mantle on Elisha. This signified he was the next prophet to take Elijah's place. Yet he told him "Go back, for what have I done to you."

Why did Elijah say this? Because he wanted Elisha to know for himself that he was called by God and not by man. Elisha had to know that he was called, not Elijah knowing for him.

Even when things are not going well, you still have to know for yourself that God called you. If man calls and appoints you, then man will have to keep you, which is impossible! But if God calls you and appoints you, God will anoint you and keep all that He has entrusted in your care. Paul explains it this way: "I am not ashamed for I know whom I have believed and am persuaded that He is able to keep what I have committed to Him until that day" (2 Tim. 1:12).

It is not God's responsibility to know your purpose; it's yours. You are responsible to recognize the deep desire birthed in your spirit. The discovering and choice of destiny is up to you.

You have the choice of discovering and fulfilling your purpose and returning to your Maker and Creator. Or, you can choose not to seek or discover your purpose, complete your mission, reject God and go to your master, the devil.

True, God is the Maker and Creator of everyone, but He is not Master of everyone. Paul said in Romans 6:16, "Whom you serve is your master, whether it be God or the devil."

Jesus told the Pharisees in John 8:44, "Ye are of your father the devil..." Paul later said in Romans 8:9, "If anyone does not have the Spirit of Christ abiding on the inside of him, he does not belong to Him." If you do not have the Spirit of God in you, then you do not belong to Christ. Once you enter this world, the power of choice is up to you to discover your purpose, complete your mission, finish your course and return back to God.

Remember, God is not trying to get anyone to know your calling or purpose but you.

"*Before I formed thee in the belly I knew thee; and before thou camest forth out of the womb I sanctified thee, and I ordained thee a prophet unto the nations.*"

—JEREMIAH 1:5

Chapter 4

Birthing a Ministry

One day I was in my kitchen washing dishes, thinking about everything I was facing. The ministry God had given me was about to be birthed yet there was so much against me. Standing there at the sink I heard God ask, "Bridget, what tells on you, but doesn't talk?" I laughed out loud because I had no idea what the answer was.

I answered: "Please tell me Lord because I truly don't know." He whispered and said, "Time! Bridget, time doesn't talk, but time will tell and all will know that your ministry is truly of God."

My ministry was there before I was even conceived. It was foreordained and predestined by God. I had carried it for thirty-one years and it was time for it to be birthed—to come forth. I say thirty-one years because I realized that when I was born, I was born with a purpose. That purpose came with me in my mother's womb. The calling was there even before I was born.

Jeremiah 1:5 says that before God formed you in your mother's womb, He knew you. Before you were born, He sanctified you. He ordained you to be a prophet to the nations.

By my being a pastor, the calling was there all the time. I had to discover and recognize it. At the age of six I discovered that I was called to be a teacher of the gospel. I would say to my mother, "One day I'm going to be a preacher. I'm going to teach this Bible."

Having walked with the Lord for many years, God in time revealed and unfolded the fullness of my calling. All I wanted to do was talk about Jesus and read my Bible. Many people, including my mother, did not understand this. I realize now that those who tried to suppress my urge to preach God's Word really did not understand much about spiritual things.

In 2 Kings 4, Elisha did not know that the Shunammite lady's baby had died. He was the one God used to prophesy to her that she was going to have a child. When the child died, God hid that from him. God does not reveal in the spirit everything to everybody.

Understand that the gifts of the Holy Spirit are in operation not as man wills, but as God wills, according to 1 Corinthians 12:11. When the Shunammite lady ran to Elisha for help, to let him know her baby had died, he sent his servant, Gehazi, to run and meet her and say, "It is well with you." She answered and said, "It is well" (2 Kin. 4:28).

The Bible says, "And when she came to the man of God at the hill, she caught him by the feet: but Gehazi came near to thrust her away. And the man of God said, Let her alone; for her soul is in deep distress and the Lord has hidden it from me and has not told me" (2 Kin. 4:27). As I stated earlier, God does not reveal in the spirit everything to everybody.

One thing the mother knew was that all was well—even in death. Yes, God will withhold from showing others your purpose and calling, even those of great reputation, because God wants *you* to know.

People in general are so quick to point out all the many faults they see in others. But such an attitude actually prevents them from seeing God. Man looks at the outer appearance, but God sees the heart. Many people told me that my calling to be a pastor could not be, simply because I was a woman. Not only was I a woman, but a young woman of thirty-one years of age. At that time, May 1994, I was the youngest woman pastor in the city of Baton Rouge, Louisiana. God had hid so much from them.

Most individuals judge from the outside, the natural standpoint. Yes, in the natural, I was young, but in the spirit I was mature. God said to me, "Bridget, there are many people in the natural who are older than you, but in the spirit, you are older than they. When they were in their 30s and hanging out at bars, you were just six years old and on your knees praying, developing a relationship, a line of open communication and fellowship with Me."

Even though in the natural I was younger, in God's eyes and in His reality, I was older in the spirit.

Paul told Timothy, "Let no man despise thy youth; but be thou an example to the believers, in word, in conduct, in love, in spirit, in faith and in purity" (1 Tim. 4:12). You can be young in age, but mature spiritually, or old in age and immature spiritually.

Paul said in Hebrews 5:12, "For when for the time ye ought to be teachers, ye have need that one teach you again which be the first principles of the oracles of God; and are become such as have need of milk, and not of strong meat."

God had hid the many years I had walked with Him, and the years of training, trials and tribulations I had gone through. I had developed a strong discipline in praying and studying God's Word—for hours and hours, day after day. Sometimes morning, noon and night, I would pour over my Bible.

Before God labels anything, the product first has to be tested. God first calls you and then trains you. Finally, He commissions you to go. Many people want to be called and then commissioned, but few want to be trained. God will never call and commission anyone unless they go through the discipline of a training process.

Oftentimes such training entails going through some "wilderness" experiences. But that's where God trains us—when we're in the wilderness. Those tests, trials and tribulations cause the gifting deep inside us to be perfected. This also enables us to grow and become strong.

Experience brings about wisdom. You can only teach, preach and testify according to the personal accountability you've experienced with God. You cannot teach or preach something you do not know. God is in the "knowing" business. He wants you to truly *know* He is the Deliverer, the Healer and the Provider. God wants you to know!

Your faith has to be tested and refined to prove that it is strong and pure. Peter writes: "Wherein ye greatly rejoice, though now for a season, if need be, ye are in heaviness through manifold temptations: That the trial of your faith, being much more precious than of gold that perisheth, though it be tried with fire, might be found unto praise and honour and glory at the appearing of Jesus Christ" (1 Pet. 1:6-7).

Your faith has to be strong because many believers and nonbelievers will fight against you. So, go through what you have to go through. All the adversities you face are not just for you. Always know that they are for somebody else as well. God is preparing you for great works. All that you go through will work out for your good at the end, especially for those "who are called according to his purpose."

"And Enoch walked with God: and he was not; for God took him."

—GENESIS 5:24

Chapter 5

A Personal Walk With God

Throughout the years of my walk with Christ, I have encountered many great experiences. At age six, I was saved and baptized. After that, all I wanted to do was talk about Jesus and read my Bible. At one point, my dear mother took away my Bible for fear I was going to go insane.

I can remember one time as a youngster when I was by myself, eating a meal. I began talking to God and was actually angry at Him for not eating from my spoon (I was very young at the time!). I had grown to have such faith in God that I knew He could do whatever He wanted to. I would pray and talk to God all the time.

God was so real to me that I would get angry when He showed me dreams that concerned things I had prayed and talked to Him about. I would get disgruntled because I knew I had the faith to believe He was going to do what I asked, and He did not need to show me a dream. Even as a child I had a rock-solid, unwavering faith in God.

I can remember scolding God and asking Him, "Why did you show me this or that when you knew I believed You and Your Word?" I knew He was hearing and honoring what I said, and in Him and His Word alone I would believe. I would get upset because I wanted Him to know that I believed even without a dream.

One thing I have learned over the years is that you should never make visions and dreams the foundation on what you are believing God for. Always let the Word of God be your foundation. Even when you do not have visions and dreams, you will always have the Word. "Heaven and earth will pass away, but my words will by no means pass away" (Matt. 24:35).

Peter says, "We also have a more sure word of prophecy; whereunto ye do well that ye take heed, as unto a light that shineth in a dark place" (2 Pet. 1:19). Meaning, God's Word is a prophecy on its own. If you have the faith to believe God's Word, then God has the power to demonstrate what you are believing Him for. Scripture will come to pass on its own if you believe what it says.

Throughout my childhood my relationship with God continued to grow into a close, intimate walk. I remember praying every day, three times a day. God was so real to me, I just had a desire to talk to Him as much as I could. At night I would pray diligently and Mother used to come and shake me and say, "Bridget are you sleeping?" because I would pray quietly so she couldn't hear me. And I would tell her how I was praying, talking to my Lord.

During my teen years, my relationship with God grew even stronger. Just about every day, I would walk down our dusty old road in the evening to meet and talk with God after a long day at school. I had it in my heart to be with God and in His presence. As I walked down that road, God's presence would come mightily upon me. It was so strong that it seemed as if I were in another world. What an awesome experience!

In 1978, my mother was hospitalized—her doctor had determined that she was physically exhausted and needed a great deal of rest. She had been a single mom for many years, raising me and my twelve siblings by herself. We lived in Clinton, Louisiana, where she worked at an area hospital.

Many people came by to pamper my mom and help her get well. There was just so much love—I know it was God's favor upon her. I was sixteen years old at the time and she asked me to take care of her personal business. I was to cash her checks, pay the bills, and deposit the rest in her bank account.

But I never got to do that. I lost the envelope containing $1,000 in cash. The only items in the envelope were the money and my mom's driver's license. I had stopped off at a clothing store, went to the register to pay for the items and behold— no envelope, no money! I had lost it and did not know where.

Normally, incidents such as this will cause you to lose all thoughts. But the presence of God arose so mightily upon me that I heard a voice say, "Don't worry, you'll get it back," and a peace swept my heart.

According to Philippians 4:7: "And the peace of God, which passeth all understanding, shall keep your hearts and minds through Christ Jesus." The peace of God will not only let you know that all is well, but it will also let you know you have God's permission on whatever you may be asking Him. If you ever want to know whether you have God's permission on anything, wait to see if He gives you a peace about it. The peace of God will surpass or go beyond your understanding. It lets you know all is well. My mother is a woman of strong faith. When I told her what had happened, her response was, "Bridget, don't worry. The Lord is my shepherd and I shall not want. If it be God's perfect will, then I'll get the money back. If not, then I won't." She said no more about the subject; that was it.

Well, I knew it had to be God's perfect will for that money to turn up because it was our entire living expense for the month. For six days the money remained lost, but on the seventh day a policeman called my mother and said, "Mrs. Barnes, we have an envelope at the police department with $1,000 and your driver's license inside. Come by and pick it up whenever you can."

My mother and I shouted and gave God the glory! If God said it, He will do it. If He spoke it, He will bring it to pass. Train yourself to believe God and His Word alone. Know that the Word of God is a sure prophecy on its own.

The Spirit World

"And the very God of peace sanctify you wholly; and I pray God your whole spirit and soul and body be preserved blameless unto the coming of our Lord Jesus Christ."

—1 THESSALONIANS 5:23

Chapter 6

Your Spirit Is the Real You

Many years ago there was a deep desire birthed down in my heart (spirit) that I was going to be a teacher of the gospel. That desire stayed in my heart.

One way of recognizing your purpose is to notice what deep desire has been born inside of you—in your spirit. God has put that desire there so you can recognize your calling or purpose. It is in that inner being—our spirit—where God lives, lead, directs, instructs and orders our footsteps. According to 1 John 2:20, "God in you will let you know all things." Anything that concerns you or pertains to you, you will know it. God communicates with man's spirit. You see, the spirit is the real you. Paul says, "And the very God of peace sanctify you wholly; and I pray God your whole spirit and soul and body be preserved blameless unto the coming of our Lord Jesus Christ" (1 Thess. 5:23).

Start listening to your spirit. There will be a witness in your spirit from the Holy Ghost of what God has called you to do. You will know it from the inside, and the Holy Ghost will bear witness to it because He only bears witness to the truth. If it is not the truth, He will not bear witness to it.

Romans 8:16 says, "The Spirit Himself bears witness with our spirit that we are the children of God." Only when we make true confessions, ask forgiveness for our sins, and accept Jesus Christ as our Lord and personal Savior will the Holy Spirit come in, abide in us, and bear witness that we are children of God.

"*The spirit of man is the candle of the Lord, searching all the inward parts of the belly.*"

—PROVERBS 20:27

Chapter 7

The Spirit of Man

Man is a "tri-being." That is, we each possess a spirit, a soul and a body. (See 1 Thessalonians 5:23.) When Jesus said, "Marvel not, you must be born again" (John 3:7), He was speaking of the spirit of man. This new birth, the rebirth of a human spirit, means our spirit has to be reborn. When we are born again, there are two things we receive from God: God's nature, which is love, and His life, which is eternal.

Our original nature had to be changed; we had to be transformed and converted. When we receive Christ into our life, we receive the very nature and life of God. The Spirit of God comes to live in our spirit—it's a change that takes place spiritually.

This is how God the Father and God the Son live in us by His precious Holy Spirit. They are three in one. Even though they are three separate entities, they are also one. They have always been and they will always be in one accord and in agreement with each other.

Many people say, "God lives in my heart," but what they are really saying is, "God lives in my spirit." Your heart is part of your body. Yes, your spirit is in your body, but God does not live in your hands or feet, or your soul—God lives in your spirit. Your spirit is the part of you that contacts God. It is your spirit that communicates with God.

If God lived in your fleshly heart, when medical doctors performed an organ transplant on you, they would give you to someone else. Not so! No one can give you to someone else because only you can give away the organ that is part of the body, but you cannot give away your spirit.

Your spirit is the real you. Your spirit and your soul are eternal. Peter calls the spirit of man the hidden man (1 Pet. 3:4). Real beauty comes from within. Peter was simply saying don't spend so much time on the outward man (body) but the inward (spirit). Paul calls the spirit the inward man (2 Cor. 4:16).

Many people are looking for the "supernatural," but the real and true supernatural is actually in them. They seek for a prophet and the prophet is in them. Jesus became your high priest, king and prophet. He is in you! If you just learn to spend time with Him through prayer, meditation, reading and studying the Bible, you will find out that He speaks quite often. Not only will He give you the answer, He also will uncover, reveal and unfold whatever needs to be in your life.

If you are spending dedicated, qualified time with God and have an intimate relationship with Him, then God calls you His friend (John 15:15) and will guide you and tell you of things to come (John 16:13). Why would God have to call someone across town to speak to you, when you already have—or can have—fellowship, relationship and direct communication with Him?

If God would speak to anybody first, it is going to be you. If He does choose to send you a word through another individual, it will be a word of confirmation concerning something He's already told you. God will speak a word to you in due season for whatever reason, or for whatever you are going through.

People need to stop searching for *a word* from

someone else and start searching *the Word*—the Word of God. The Bible is fulfilled prophecy on its own. If we would only believe what God's Word says, it will come to pass. Peter said, "We have also a more sure word of prophecy..." (2 Pet. 1:19), which means that the Word of God found in the Bible is surer and more accurate than any vision or dream.

Throughout the Bible there are examples of God speaking into certain situations two or more times. I've seen it happen repeatedly in my life and ministry that first, He speaks to the individual. This can be through an inward witness, a small still voice or a vision, dream or prophecy. If God chooses to speak through another person, it will be to confirm what He's already said.

People are wrong to seek out a prophet for a word from God. In fact, we insult our heavenly Father when we overlook the fact that He lives in us, ready to speak into our lives. The Bible promises us that God knows all things and will let us know all things. "But you have an anointing from the Holy one and you know all things" (1 John 2:20).

God will show you things to come, according to John 16:13. He may not come when you want Him to, but thanks be to God, He's always on time! It may seem that He's a last-minute God, but He's still on time. Sometimes it may seem that He's all you've got, but He's everything you need.

Throughout the Old Testament the anointing rested only upon the kings, priests, and prophets. The prophets were God's mouthpiece. Thanks to God, the anointing will not only come upon us, but the anointing is also with us. God is in us. He will speak to you Himself.

According to the New Testament, we have received a better covenant with better promises. Scripture says in 1 John 2:27, "But the anointing which ye have received of him abides in you." Again, in 1 John 2:20, it reads, "And you will know all things." It is a joy to know that someone else won't know for you, but you will know for yourself.

The Word of God is a prophecy on its own. If you have enough faith to believe God, then God has enough power to demonstrate whatever you are believing Him for. Receive what the Word of God is saying and it will come to pass. Jesus said in Mark 11:23, "Whoever says...and does not doubt in his heart, but believes that those things he says will be done, he will have whatever he says."

Proverbs 20:27 says, "The spirit of man is the candle of the Lord, searching all the inner depths of his heart." The word "heart," used here, is interchangeable with spirit. Again, God does not live in the actual heart chamber because that is part of your physical body. God lives in your spirit. The real you is your spirit. When a heart donor dies in Christ, his spirit goes to heaven—only his natural heart is given to someone else.

The Holy Spirit is the candle—the light—that is in our spirit. It is God's Holy Spirit in us who guides, leads, directs, instructs and orders our footsteps. The Holy Spirit was sent to convict and not condemn us for our sins.

According to 1 John 3:20, our own spirit can condemn us. Our spirit has a voice, it's called our conscience. Your own spirit will talk to you and remind you of your guilt and make you feel condemned.

Remember, when you were born again, you received the very nature of God. Your new nature knows not to do wrong, nor does it want to. But when you yield to the flesh, you will fall to sin.

Keep in mind that if you happen to fall, do not wallow in your mess. Get up, repent and get back on track with God. You have an Advocator—your heavenly Attorney, your Defender—who is the One pleading your case to God the Father. His name is Jesus! First John 1:9 says, "If we confess our sins, He is faithful and just to forgive us our sins, and to cleanse us from all unrighteousness."

God lives in you. He lives in your spirit and will lead you by His Spirit. We have to learn to spend sufficient time on a daily basis with God, in prayer and in His Word. This is the only way to become more sensitive to the Holy Spirit. He is God in us. Everyday we need to have relationship, communication and fellowship with God.

Paul said in 1 Corinthians 3:16, "Know ye not that ye are the temple of God, and that the Spirit of God dwelleth in you?" First John 2:27 says, "But the anointing which ye have received of him abideth in you."

The anointing is the very presence, power and authority of God. You demean God when you look to another person to lead you, guide you, direct and instruct you, and order your footsteps, especially since God is in you.

If you are spending time with God on a daily basis, who do you think God will speak to first? You! Again I say, if God chooses to give you a word through another, then let it be God's doing, and not yours. If God chooses to do so, it is only going to be a confirmation of what He's already said to you.

There is one thing I've realized that hurts very badly, and that is when I see the devil successfully fooling even God's own elect. I've seen strong, dedicated Christians seek sorcerers, fortune tellers and false prophets. It causes such a pain deep within my spirit. Believers do this because they think that the person on the other end of that 1-900 psychic hotline—or whatever—can give them a word.

One thing they must realize, however, is that this is not a word from the Lord, but from demons. What many people don't realize is that demons can prophesy too.

Paul writes, "But one and the same Spirit works all

these things, distributing to each one individually as He wills" (1 Cor. 12:11). He's referring to the gifts of the Holy Spirit. God moves, speaks and manifests as He will, not when your money wants Him to. You cannot pay God to speak, move or manifest just because you want Him to! If someone is paying to hear a word from a sorcerer or fortune teller, they actually will be hearing from demons—not God.

In 1 Samuel 28, Saul visited a medium, also known as a sorcerer or fortune teller. Saul was tired, weary, oppressed, depressed and looking for an answer. Being deceived by the devil, he went to the fortune teller for the answer.

As you read this passage, notice that Saul disguised himself by wearing different clothes. He knew it was forbidden by God to seek sorcerers and fortune tellers. However, the demon spirit recognized that it was Saul in disguise. The woman sorcerer did not know it was Saul, but the demon spirit dwelling inside her did. That demon spirit also spoke and told Saul certain things that were to come to pass. The things that were spoken did come to pass, but this is the way the devil fools even God's own elect. They do this by saying "I can help you" and "I'll tell you everything you need to know."

The Christian should realize that just because it looks right and it sounds right doesn't mean it's God. The Bible warns in Revelation 21:8 that sorcerers are among those who will "burn in the lake of fire." So remember, if you have to pay for it, it is not God because gifts from Him are absolutely free!

"There are also celestial bodies and terrestrial bodies: but the glory of the celestial is one, and the glory of the terrestrial is another."

—1 CORINTHIANS 15:40

Chapter 8

The Spirit World

The spirit world is just as real as the natural. The difference is that one is seen and the other is unseen. One is visible and the other is invisible. The Bible says in John 4:24, "God is a spirit." In 1 Thessalonians 5:23 Paul talks about man having a spirit. Jesus said in John 6:63 that His words are spirit.

Hence, we see that there is a spirit world. The words you speak are spirit. The air you breathe is spirit. We need to realize that the spirit world does exist, and we need to learn how to function and operate spiritually. We must learn how to walk in the spirit.

The writer in Galatians 5:16, vividly points this out when he remarks, "I say then, Walk in the Spirit." When you walk by faith, you are walking in the Spirit.

In the natural we had to learn to walk, talk, read, drive and so on. Likewise, spiritually we have to learn to function and operate by simply speaking God's Word and walking by faith.

Paul says, "There are also celestial bodies (heavenly) and terrestrial bodies (earthly); but the glory of the celestial is one, and the glory of the terrestrial is another" (1 Cor. 15:40). He also mentions in 1 Corinthians 15:44, "It is sown a natural body, it is raised a spiritual body. There is a natural body and a spiritual body."

There is also a natural world and a spiritual world, just as there is natural food and spiritual food. There are natural laws and there are spiritual laws. The spirit world does exist; it is a reality.

In the natural you look like your earthly parents, but in the spirit you look like your heavenly parents...the Trinity—they are spirit! You see, Jesus came from that spirit world as did Jeremiah and you and I.

John writes, "In the beginning was the Word, and the Word was with God and the Word was God" (John 1:1). Before Jesus was given the name Jesus, He was first the Word, the Word is spirit. What I am emphasizing is that Jesus was spirit, living in the spirit world with Father God.

In John 6:63, Jesus said, "The words that I speak are spirit and life." You see, God's Word is *spirit* and it also is *life*. Jesus *was* the Word and the Word was made flesh. He came to give eternal life to all mankind.

Jesus laid aside all His pre-incarnated glory to come down and redeem man. He laid aside His omnipresence (being everywhere at the same time), His omnipotence (all-powerful), His omniscience (all-knowing), and became flesh. In the flesh He was limited. He walked so far and got tired; therefore, He had to rest. When He got thirsty, He needed water. When He was hungry, He needed food. He only had two hands to reach multitudes of people.

He had to be endowed with power from on high. In other words, He had to receive the spirit baptism. He did no signs, wonders or miracles; nor did He begin His ministry until He was endowed with power. That is the way He overcame all spiritual satanic forces on earth. He was empowered by the Holy Ghost. This illustrates the fact that many can live on this earth in the flesh and be endowed with power from on high and dominate over all spiritual darkness.

In Ephesians 1:3 Paul talked about this spirit world called heavenly places. Paul said, "Blessed be the God and Father of our Lord Jesus Christ, who hath blessed us with all spiritual blessings in heavenly places in Christ." There are different levels of heaven. Earth, air, the constellations, and God's throne are all different levels of heaven. God's throne is the heavenly place where Father God dwells, where Jesus came from, and where Jeremiah was before he was conceived in his mother's womb and made flesh.

As previously stated, before Jesus was given the name Jesus, He was first the Word. John 1:1 says, "In the beginning was the Word, and the Word was with God, and the Word was God." The question is: with God where? In the heavenly place, the spirit world.

Jeremiah 1:5 says, "Before I formed thee in the belly I knew thee; before thou camest forth out of the womb I sanctified thee; and I ordained thee a prophet unto the nations."

The word *before* means preceding in time, in front, or ahead. Now the question is, if God knew Jeremiah beforehand or ahead, where did He know him first? Or should we ask, where was he first known? Where was Jeremiah before he became flesh?

The answer is that God first knew Jeremiah in the spirit. Jeremiah was spirit before he became flesh. He lived in the spirit world called the heavenly. He was born spirit first. He was first spiritually ordained a prophet before he became one naturally.

In Luke 1:35, the Holy Spirit impregnated Mary, Jesus' mother. The Holy Spirit conceived Jesus. His was a spiritual birth that took place first, before the natural birth. He was conceived spiritually, but born naturally. Just like Jesus' birth was spiritual, so must all mankind have a spiritual birth, meaning you must be born again. There is a natural birth and a spiritual birth.

Jesus told Nicodemus in John 3:3, "most assuredly I say unto you unless one is born again, you cannot see the kingdom of God." Nicodemus asked the question, "How can a man be born again when he is old? Can he enter a second time in his mother's womb?"

Jesus answers, "Unless one is born of the water, they will not see God." The word *water*, used here, means God's Word because water baptism does not save anyone. Water baptism is a symbol of Jesus' death, burial and resurrection. You can go down into the water a "dry devil" and come up a wet one. Just as Simon, the sorcerer, did in Acts 8.

The Word is spirit and life. The Word gives life and produces light. In 1 Peter 1:23 it says, "Being born again, not of corruptible seed, but of incorruptible, by the word of God, which liveth and abideth for ever."

Jesus said in John 3:6-7 (parenthetical remarks are mine), "That which is flesh is flesh (speaking of the natural birth) and that which is born of the Spirit is spirit (speaking of the spiritual birth). Do not marvel; (let this not be a surprise to you) you must be born again."

How is a person born again? They have to be born again spiritually. The spirit of man has to be changed, converted, transformed and renewed by the power of the Holy Ghost. Simply by accepting Jesus Christ into your heart and life, and by recognizing Him as Savior will be the beginning of a new life. It is called the new birth, which is the rebirth of a human spirit. It is the beginning of a new beginning.

You see, when we were born into this world, we were born into sin. David said in Psalm 51:5, "Behold, I was shapen in iniquity; and in sin did my mother conceive me." We were born with the nature of the devil. So, spiritually we were a child of the devil. That is why Jesus said we all must be born again. Otherwise, we will not enter the kingdom of God. Man's nature has to be changed in order for him to enter the kingdom of God.

Gehazi, the servant of Elisha the prophet, had the opportunity to experience looking into the spirit world.

In 2 Kings 6:13, during the time when the king of Syria was making war against Israel, the king of Syria took counsel with his servants and told them his camp would be in certain places. And God revealed each time to Elisha the plan of the enemy. From there, Elisha would warn the king of Israel of the enemy's plan.

The king of Syria was greatly troubled by this. He called his servants and asked them, "Will you not show me which of us is for the king of Israel?" One of the servants said, "None, my lord, but Elisha, the prophet who is in Israel, tells the king of Israel the words that you speak in your bedroom." Therefore, the king of Syria sent horses and chariots and a great army to the city Dothan to bring back the prophet Elisha.

When the servant of the man of God arose early and went out, there was an army surrounding the city with horses and chariots. And Gehazi, Elisha's servant, said to him, "Master! What shall we do?" Elisha answered and said, "Do not fear, for those who are with us are more than those who are with them." Elisha saw in the spirit that there were more for them than there was against them. Elisha prayed to God that his servant Gehazi's eyes would be opened to see in the spirit world. When God opened the eyes of Gehazi to see in the spirit world, he saw the army of God was so much greater than the army of the king of Syria. The scripture says, "Behold the mountain was full of horses and chariots of fire all around Elisha."

There were more horses and chariots in the spirit for Elisha than there were for the king of Syria in the natural.

"Now faith is the substance of things hoped for, the evidence of things not seen."

—HEBREWS 11:1

Chapter 9

Receiving It First
in the Spirit

Faith is a spirit, meaning it is unseen. Faith is simply acting on the Word of God. Faith says everything the Word of God says. Remember that according to John 6:63, God's words are spirit. Hebrews 11:1 says, "Faith is the substance of things hoped for and the evidence of things not seen."

As you can see, faith will manifest the substance of that for which you are hoping for. The Amplified version of the Bible puts it like this, "Faith is the assurance, the confirmation, the title deed of things we hope for, being the proof of things we do not see."

When we purchase items such as automobiles, homes or land, we receive titles that are official documents declaring us as the legal owner.

Well, faith works in a similar way. When we believe the promises of God—whether it be spiritual or physical blessings—by faith we already have them. Faith says, "I am your title deed, confirmation, and your assurance of that which you are believing God for." You have in your hand the "paper," which is the Word of

God, sealed with the blood of Jesus.

As believers walking in faith we have been approved for all the blessings because Jesus paid the ultimate price for us to have them. This is supported in Paul's writings when he says, "For all the promises of God in him are yea, and in him Amen" (2 Cor. 1:20). Thus, according to Mark, "Whatever things you ask when you pray, believe that you receive them and ye shall have them" (Mark 11:24).

Let's look at the word *receive*. If I have *already* received them, *where* did I receive them? In my spirit! They are first spirit, lying in a place called the heavenly. According to Ephesians 1:3, "Blessed be the God and Father of our Lord Jesus Christ, who hath blessed us with all spiritual blessings in heavenly places in Christ."

Romans 4:17 says, "Speak those things that do not exist as though they do exist." Where do they first exist? In the spirit! You receive it first in the spirit, then the Holy Ghost manifests it in the natural. By faith I have what I prayed for already. It is unseen first because it is in the spirit, but faith says I already have it. I am just waiting for the Holy Ghost to manifest it in the natural.

Faith always sees the answer, and I can see it through the eyes of faith. Faith says, "I am your title deed, your confirmation, and your assurance of whatever you are believing God for." Praise Him for it; you already have it!

You first receive from God in the spirit; then the Holy Ghost will manifest it in the natural. Your faith will cause all the blessings that are in the heavenly to be manifested in the natural. Faith can get you from earth to glory. It is very important that we learn to operate spiritually—to tap in on the world called heavenly by simply walking by faith.

Paul says, "For we walk by faith, not by sight" (2 Cor. 5:7). Faith is unseen, sight is seen. One is spiritual, the other natural. Sight is your sensibility realm, which consists of your ability to hear, see, smell, taste and feel. Faith is how we go up in the spirit world and pull down our needs, wants and desires.

Ephesians 1:3, which I already mentioned, confirms this: "Blessed be the God and Father of our Lord Jesus Christ, who hath blessed us with all spiritual blessings in heavenly places in Christ." Notice God is not the only one blessed. Paul says that we are blessed, too. We are blessed with all spiritual blessings in the heavenly.

In 1 Corinthians 3:21, Paul says that God has given us all things: "therefore let no man glory in men. For all things are yours." I interpret that as meaning we must learn how to go up and receive all these things, natural or spiritual.

Paul said, "We are blessed with all spiritual blessings." Notice how all these things are first spirit and in the spirit world. Paul says, "Blessed be the God, the Father of our Lord and Saviour, Jesus Christ, who has (meaning it already has been done) blessed us with every spiritual blessing (first they are spiritual in the heavenly).

Remember, when you are walking by faith, you are walking in the spirit. Faith causes that which is in the spirit world to be manifested in the natural. You may have a "symptom of sickness" that's ailing your body (I believe Christians don't have sickness—they just have symptoms!).

Jesus Himself took our infirmities and bore our sicknesses in His own body. We also know Jesus died so that we might be healed. Remember, first it is in the spirit that we receive our healing, and then the Spirit of God, by faith, manifests it in the natural. This is also the way it works with everything else you are believing God for. Remember John 6:63: "God's word is spirit and life." We must believe God's Word.

God already has blessed you according to Ephesians 1:3. Your faith is going to cause whatever blessings that is spiritual in the heavenly to be manifested in the natural. Peter says, "God has given to us all things that pertain to life and godliness through the knowledge of

Him who called us by glory and virtue" (2 Pet. 1:3).

Let's look at the word *all* in that verse. God already has given us *all* things pertaining to life and godliness—whether it be natural or spiritual. God already has blessed you with *all* things.

Mark 11:24 says, "Whatsoever things you ask for when you pray, believe that you receive them, and you shall have them." Perhaps it is your house, car, healing or personal finances that need a touch from God. Take heart, that the "answer" is first in the spirit and then you receive it in the natural. It is spiritual, in the "heavenly place"! Faith allows or permits you to go up to the heavenly and receive all your blessings and pull them down to earth.

According to Romans 4:17, "We have to call those things that do not exist as though they do." In other words, those things that do not exist in the natural at the moment, do already exist in the spirit. So again, speak the Word of God by faith. Faith sees the answer. Believing accepts it as real and true. It gives you a divine ownership to something that you know is yours already! Your faith will cause that which does not exist to exist. It will cause that which is in the spirit to be manifested in the natural.

Second Peter 1:4 points out that God has "given unto us exceeding great and precious promises." However, without knowledge of the Word of God, we would not know about these promises God has given us. God promises that no matter what we are going through, we will triumph in all things.

You are victorious. You are more than a conqueror and an overcomer. You are already healed, delivered and prosperous. Notice sometimes when you encounter trials in this life, you do not feel as if you triumph, nor do you *feel* victorious, healed, delivered or prosperous. Well, God did not tell you to *feel* as if you triumphed or to *feel* victorious, healed, delivered or prosperous. He says, "Know that you are"!

Remember you are a faith creature. You do not have to *feel* it, just *know* it because God and His Word says so.

You do not walk by sight, you walk by faith. Remember, sight is your sensibility realm—your five senses of smell, taste, hearing, sight and feeling. All of these can throw you off. Just because you do not feel it or see it in the natural, you may think God has not done it.

God said in Exodus 33:17, "I will do this thing." He also said in 2 Kings 3:18, "...this is but a light thing in the sight of the Lord..." Not only has God said it, God has done it! The "done" part means it is already done; the "do it" part means He is going to manifest that thing!

But, it is first done in the spirit. When you triumph, it is first in the spirit. You are first victorious in the spirit. Then the Holy Spirit will manifest it in the natural by faith.

Women in the Ministry

"So God created man in his own image, in the image of God created he him; male and female created he them."

—GENESIS 1:27

Chapter 10

Women in the Ministry

For too long I have heard too many women ministers classify themselves in the same category as animals! They do this when they say, "If God can make a donkey talk, He also can use a woman." However, I am here to tell you that women are not in the same class with animals! We are in the same class with God, meaning spirit.

Paul says in 1 Thessalonians 5:23, "And the very God of peace sanctify you wholly; and I pray God your whole spirit and soul and body be preserved blameless unto the coming of our Lord Jesus Christ."

You see, man is a spirit who possesses a soul and lives in a body. God said in Genesis 1:26, "Let us make man in our image, after our likeness." According to John 4:24, "God is a spirit"—therefore, the image of God is spirit.

Here, the reference to the word *man* means "all mankind"—regardless of whether you are male or female. If we are made in the image and likeness of God, Scripture says it is only by spirit. God sees us as spirit, not as male or female and not as a mammal.

Animals have only a soul, but man has spirit, soul and body. There is no life for an animal after death because they have only a soul. But for man it is different. Man is a spirit just like God. Man has a spirit, possesses a soul and lives in a body. Therefore, there is life after death for man because the spirit is eternal. In the natural, one may look like his mother and father; but in the supernatural we all are just like God—spirit.

Genesis 1:27 says, "God created man in his own image, (meaning spirit) in the image of God created he him; male and female created he them." Notice the word *man*. Keep in mind that *man* is defined as *all* mankind, regardless of sex. God does not see us as male, female, or even as color—He sees us as spirit.

In John 6:63, Jesus said, "...the words that I speak unto you, they are spirit, and they are life." Even God's Word is *spirit* and produces life. As I mentioned earlier, before Jesus was given the name Jesus, He was first the Word and the word became flesh (see John 1:14). A woman, Mary, carried the word in her womb, and the word that she carried produced life. It was Jesus that brought eternal life to all mankind.

Now, if a woman can carry the word in her womb, what makes it so hard for us to believe that God can use a woman to carry that same word in her heart (meaning spirit)?

It is true, according to Scripture, that the same life—the word—that was conceived in Mary's womb is now being conceived in man's heart whether they be male or female, man or woman. For Jesus is the word.

Again, in John 1:1 we find, "...the Word was with God, and the Word was God." Jesus was the word and the word was carried in the womb of a woman. Now the same word is carried in the hearts of men *and women* today!

As we study Genesis 1:26 and verse 28, we find that God gave dominion to mankind. They both—man and woman—were given, and have been given, spiritual authority by God to rule over the power of the enemy. They both are to rule over spiritual darkness, satanic forces and over all the works of the enemy by using the Word of God. Realizing this, the only things the devil is to take from believers are commands and orders. He is not to take our families, loved ones, finances, and so on!

I stated earlier my dismay when I hear women ministers classify themselves with animals. "If God can make a donkey talk or if He can make a rooster crow then He can certainly use me!" No, God made the donkey talk because He wanted to. Likewise, He made the rooster crow because He wanted the rooster to crow.

However, God did not tell women to crow. If He wanted them to crow, He would have made them a rooster. God called women to preach—not to animals—but to people! He called them to minister, teach and preach the gospel, the uncompromised Word of God.

The word *preach* means to "proclaim" the Word of God, and the word *gospel* means "good news." I firmly believe that God is calling women to proclaim the good news of the gospel to all mankind—men, women, boys and girls.

Matthew 28:1-8 vividly illustrates how two women, Mary Magdalene and the other Mary, were the first ones to proclaim the good news that, "Jesus is not dead, but He is alive." It was women who proclaimed His death, burial and resurrection!

Not only was a woman the first to carry the word, a woman delivered the word and then preached the word. When the angel of the Lord descended from heaven and rolled back the stone from the sepulcher, it was not rolled back to let Jesus out; but to let the women in to *testify*, to *preach* and to *proclaim* the Good News. Jesus is not dead—He is alive! The empty tomb is proof! The women were given commands by the angel of God to go and proclaim the news—to tell the disciples that, "He has risen from the dead."

"But every woman that prayeth or prophesieth with her head uncovered dishonoureth her head: for that is even all one as if she were shaven."

—1 CORINTHIANS 11:5

Chapter 11

The Simple Gift of Prophecy

John 4:24 scripture says, "God is a Spirit..." Genesis 1:27 says, "God created man in his own image, in the image of God..." We are made in the image of God meaning spirit. Man is a spirit, possesses a soul and lives in a body. (See 1 Thessalonians 5:23.) John 6:63 says, "The words I have spoke to you [God's Word] are spirit and they are life." Therefore, just like God we are a spirit, speaking spiritual words to edify, exhort and to comfort.

Ephesians 4:11 explains that Jesus gave some to be apostles, some to be prophets, some to be evangelists, and some to be pastors and teachers to equip the saints to do better work for Him in the ministry and for building up the church (the believers) to a position of strength and maturity.

God is using women and men to equip the saints and build them to a position of strength and maturity. The Bible says He gave "some" and that includes women. The word *some* was referring to the fact that God did not call every believer to stand in the office of the five-fold ministry. He also is saying that it's not just men that the fivefold gifts were given to; that would make God a respecter of persons. To show that God is no respecter of persons with His Spirit, Joel 2:28-29 states, "And it shall come to pass afterward, that I will pour out my spirit upon all flesh; and your sons and your daughters shall prophesy (preach), your old men shall dream dreams, your young men shall see visions: And also upon the servants and upon the handmaids in those days will I pour out my spirit."

Matthew 22:14 tells us that "Many are called, but few are chosen." This means everyone—man, woman, boy and girl—is called to salvation, but not everyone has been called to stand in the office of the fivefold ministry.

In this study we will be talking about the gift of prophecy, (or as I refer to it, the simple gift of prophecy), meaning edification, exhortation and comfort to the church; where one preaches, teaches, testifies or witnesses the Word of God. This gift of prophecy has no prediction or revelation with it; it simply "forth-tells" by divine inspiration. By *forth-tell*, I mean "inspiration"—speaking the Word of God. *Foretell*, on the other hand, means "predicting."

In 1 Corinthians 12:10 Paul speaks of the prophetic office of prophecy where one predicts or foretells under divine inspiration. This prophecy is one of the gifts of the Spirit and only operates according to the Holy Spirit. In verse 11, Paul writes, "But all these worketh that one and the selfsame Spirit, dividing to every man severally as he will."

In 1 Corinthians 14:1 and verse 39, Paul said, "Follow after charity, and desire spiritual gifts, but rather that ye may prophesy." In other words, Paul was saying pursue to prophesy. But he was only speaking of the simple gift of prophecy; where at all times one can exhort, comfort, and edify the body of Christ.

Paul would never have written to the church and said to pursue after something that every believer could not have. *Every* believer can have and can operate in this gift at any time, by simply speaking the Word of God. Only the Word of God can edify, exhort or comfort.

The Word of God is a prophecy all on its own. If God said it, that settles it. If He spoke it, He will bring it to pass. Bring what to pass? His Word! If you believe the Word of God, it will come to pass.

Paul said in 1 Corinthians 14:3, "But he that prophesieth speaketh unto men to edification, and exhortation, and comfort." This is the simple gift of prophecy. The next verse says, "He that speaketh in an unknown tongue edifieth himself; but he that prophesieth edifieth the church." Only God's Word can build, exalt and edify.

Verse 5 continues: "I would that ye all spake with tongues, but rather that ye prophesied: for greater is he that prophesieth than he that speaketh with tongues, except he interpret, that the church may receive edifying *not prophesy predicting someone's future.*"

Paul's wish was that we would prophesy more than we speak in tongues. However, in this passage he is speaking of the simple gift of prophecy, that a believer can pursue and operate at any time by simply speaking the Word of God.

I believe that there is much confusion in the church today because so many believers are off-balanced in their understanding of prophecy. They are pursuing the wrong type of prophecy.

Paul wrote in 1 Corinthians 11:5 that women prayed and prophesied in the church, meaning they prayed and preached in the church. In studying this chapter, you will find that men and women did the same thing in the church. They prayed and prophesied, meaning they prayed and preached the Word of God.

In verse 3 Paul says, "But I would have you know, that the head of every man is Christ; and the head of the woman is the man; and the head of Christ is God."

Verse 4 says, "Every man praying or prophesying, having his head covered, dishonoureth his head." We know that the head of man is Christ, but notice in verse 5 that the women did the same thing the men did: "But every woman that prayeth or prophesieth with her head uncovered dishonoureth her head."

Man is the head of woman. Before a woman could pray or preach, her head had to be covered, signifying her submission and honour to man.

Notice that the apostle Paul wrote to the church, not an individual. His letter was addressed to a congregation. In those days women were active in the church. They prayed and preached because the word *prophesy*, as it is used here, means "to preach." Women having their physical head covered signified that they were honoring their "head," which was their husband, or a man in general.

Even in those days God used women in mighty ways to edify, exhort and comfort the body of Christ. How? By speaking the Word of God. Only God's Word can edify, exhort or comfort.

Notice how throughout 1 Corinthians 11, Paul writes about how women were used in the early church. However, in 1 Corinthians 14, he moves to telling women to keep silent in the church. It would seem that Paul is contradicting himself, but not so.

There was a very good reason why Paul was telling the women to keep silent. He writes in 1 Corinthians 14:34, "Let your women keep silence in the churches: for it is not permitted unto them to speak; but they are commanded to be under obedience, as also saith the law."

The law Paul refers to was that women were to be submissive. He continues on this same theme in verse 35, "And if they will learn any thing, let them ask their husbands at home: for it is a shame for women to speak in the church."

During this time period in the early Christian church, women sat on one side of the church and men sat on the other. The reason Paul told these women to keep silent was because they were causing confusion in their church.

During the church service these women would yell across the aisle to where their husbands were sitting to get their attention. All the commotion was understandably causing disturbances and confusion. Paul admonishes the church that God is not the author of confusion.

He continues, "...tell the women, if they will learn anything, let them ask their husbands at home: for it is a shame for women to speak in the church." If they did, they were not being submissive to their head (which was the law of God). There was neither honor nor submission to their head. Notice Paul stated, "let them ask their husband at home." He was addressing this to married women. The married women were to keep silent in the church to avoid disturbance and confusion.

Now let's take a look at the word *prophesy* as it is used in Joel 2:28-29: "And it shall come to pass afterward that I will pour out My Spirit on all flesh; Your sons and your daughters shall prophesy (meaning preach), Your old men shall dream dreams, Your young men shall see visions. And also on My menservants and on My maidservants I will pour out My Spirit in those days."

This powerful prophecy from the book of Joel came to pass in Acts 2:1-4. "Now when the day of Pentecost was fully come, they were all with one accord in one place" (v. 1).

Pentecost was a harvest feast given once every year by the Jewish people to thank God for their harvest, grains and crops. Many people would gather together on this day for the special occasion.

Verse 2 says that, "And suddenly there came a sound from heaven, as of a rushing mighty wind, and it filled all the house where they were sitting. And there appeared unto them cloven tongues like as of fire, and it sat upon each of them. And they were all filled with the Holy Ghost and began to speak with other tongues, as the Spirit gave them utterance."

They were endowed with power from on high, strictly for service! And this included women. How do we know women were in that number? Because according to Acts 1:14: "the disciples continued with one accord in prayer and supplication, with the women, and Mary, the mother of Jesus and with His brethren." Yes, God endowed the women with power for service to get His job done.

Paul says in 2 Corinthians 3:5, "Not that we are sufficient of ourselves to think of anything as being from ourselves, but our sufficiency is from God." You see, whether it is a male or a female, any work that is done in the body of Christ, is all done by the divine ability and power of the Holy Ghost. No one can take the credit! All praise be to God!

As we look further at the word *prophesy* in Acts 21:9, we see that Philip had four virgin daughters who all prophesied. These women engaged in the simple gift of prophecy I discussed earlier. They did not stand in the prophetic office of prophecy.

Meanwhile, there was a prophet by the name of Agabus who travelled all the way from Judea to Caesarea to give Paul a prophetic word from God. God had given Agabus a word of wisdom for Paul concerning what was going to happen in the future. God had to use a prophet from Judea to bring this word to Paul because Philip's daughters operated in the simple gift of prophecy. Agabus stood in the prophetic office. He was a true prophet.

A believer not only can forth-tell, but they also can foretell. In order for one to hold the office of prophet or prophetess, they must have two of the revelation gifts in operation in their life, which are the word of wisdom and the word of knowledge or the discernment of spirits.

"And I intreat thee also, true yokefellow, help those women who laboured with me in the gospel, with Clement also, and with other my fellow labourers, whose names are in the book of life."

—PHILIPPIANS 4:3

Chapter 12

Women Laboring in the Gospel

W hen dealing with women in ministry, many see it as a natural task, but in reality it is a spiritual task. Standing before a congregation and ministering the Word of God is, in essence, a spiritual task. When a woman takes care of all the responsibilities and chores involved in running a home or working a job, that is natural.

When a woman is ministering, preaching and teaching God's Word, she becomes spiritually responsible for her flock. That's not to minimize her everyday activities at home. And even in the home she still has a certain degree of spiritual responsibility to her family, such as: raising godly children, keeping her marriage strong, and keeping peace in the home. (See Proverbs 14:1.)

Paul talks about how God gave gifts to men for the perfecting of saints for the work of the ministry and for edifying the body of Christ. (See Ephesians 4:8, 11–12.)

According to the Bible, yes, women are called to operate in the fivefold ministry gifts. God has given women the divine ability to preach, teach, evangelize, become an apostle or a pastor. It is very important to know that God is a God of principles, priorities and order. It is the order of God that when a woman is operating in the fivefold gifts in the church, she show submission to her head.

In 1 Corinthians 11: 3, Paul says, "But I want you to know that the head of every man is Christ, the head of woman is man, and the head of Christ is God." Paul also says in verse 5 that women were used mightily in the church. They were praying and preaching, but they had to show submission to their head. Whether a woman's head is her husband or another male operating in the capacity of an overseer, she must have a covering as a sign of submission.

When the time came for me to begin pastoring, the call on my life was so strong I felt as if I was pregnant and heavy with child. I just knew I had to give birth to this calling. This all came about during the time when my husband was not yet saved. I prayed, telling God I knew His Word says that He is a God of order and that a woman must show submission to her authority figure—in my case, my husband.

I told God that I did not mind answering this call, but I didn't want to enter this new arena in my life without my husband. I had been married to him for ten years and after praying that prayer I literally witnessed a miracle. God delivered my husband in his sleep and profoundly dealt with him in a dream. When he woke up the next morning, he woke up preaching.

I immediately thought of Job 33:14-18: "God will deliver man, even in his sleep, to keep back his soul from the pit and his life from perishing by the sword."

The Lord opened the eyes of my husband's spirit to understand the calling that was upon my life and the role he was to operate in my ministry. He *had* to be my head! God used my husband so mightily—he went before me to prepare and get the building ready for me to go into and do the work of the Lord.

Paul says in Philippians 4:3: "And I intreat thee also,

true yokefellow, help those women who laboured with me in the gospel, with Clement also, and with other my fellow labourers, whose names are in the book of life." Women laboured with Paul, even in Bible times. In Philippians 1:15-18, Paul writes, "Some indeed preach Christ even of envy and strife; and some also of good will: The one preach Christ of contention, not sincerely, supposing to add affliction to my bonds: But the other of love, knowing that I am set for the defense of the gospel. What then? Notwithstanding, every way, whether in pretense, or in truth, Christ is preached; and I therein do rejoice, yea, and will rejoice."

Paul was stating that it did not matter who was really preaching the gospel of Jesus Christ; his concern was that the gospel was being preached! It should not matter if the preacher, pastor, evangelist or teacher is male or female, what matters is that they preach the gospel message.

Jesus said in Luke 9:50, "Forbid him not: for he that is not against us is for us." If we are all preaching the same Jesus by the same Holy Ghost, why should we fight with one another. There's no need to concern ourselves with who is preaching the gospel. Let us get the attitude that Jesus and the apostle Paul had, and say, "My concern is not who's preaching the gospel, but that the gospel is being preached!"

In Romans 16, Paul takes time to commend and greet those laboring along with him in furthering the gospel— many of these people included women.

Phoebe was a deaconess in the church at Cenchrea. Paul admonishes his fellow believers to receive her in the Lord as "becometh saints," meaning to receive her as saints should and assist her in whatever matter she needed. Paul states that Phoebe had been a helper of many and also of himself.

Priscilla, the wife of Aquila, was a Jewish Christian deeply loyal to her faith. She laboured with Paul at Corinth and Ephesus. According to Acts 18:26, Priscilla (and Aquila) "instructed Apollos, an eloquent man, mighty in scriptures, walk more accurately in the way of God."

Mary was a woman of Rome, whom Paul declared "laboured much for us." Tryphena and Tryphosa were believed by many to be sisters who laboured much in the Lord.

Persis is who Paul called his "beloved." She laboured much in the Lord. Julia was a Christian woman who may have had some association with the imperial household. It is believed that she may have been the sister or wife to Philologus and a slave of the emperor.

In studying the New Testament, I discovered that there were many other women who labored in the early church. Mary, the mother of Jesus, has a place of honor among the women of the New Testament. As the first member of the human race to accept Christ, she stands as the first of the redeemed throughout Christian history. She is an enduring example of faith, humility and service.

Anna was a prophetess who recognized Jesus as the long-awaited Messiah. Chloe knew of divisions and dissensions within the church at Corinth. Claudia was a Christian of Rome.

Damaris, a woman of Athens, was converted under Paul's ministry. Dorcas (Tabitha), a Christian in Joppa, was raised from the dead by Peter. Elisabeth is the mother of John the Baptist.

Eunice is the mother of Timothy. Joanna provided material needs for Jesus and His disciples. Joanna also was one of the women who witnessed the empty tomb and announced Christ's resurrection to the unbelieving apostles.

Lois was the grandmother of Timothy. Lydia was a convert under Paul's ministry in Philippi. Martha and Mary were sisters of Lazarus and dear friends of Jesus.

Mary Magdalene, the woman from whom Jesus cast out seven demons, also provided for the material needs

of Jesus and His disciples. Mary also witnessed the resurrection of Jesus and was sent by Jesus to tell the
others.

Salome was the mother of Jesus' disciples James and
John. Susanna was one of the women who ministered
to Christ and His followers.

The apostle John speaks of "the elect lady" in his
second epistle. John saw the importance of acknowl-
edging the faith and laboring of this particular unnamed
woman. Further study about her reveals that she was
married; her husband isn't mentioned so perhaps she
was a widow.

She had children and it made John rejoice greatly
when he found them walking in truth and remaining
faithful to God's commandments. It is believed that she
had a church in her home and welcomed many ministers and traveling evangelists to preach there. John is
deeply pleased to be able to commend the family. It
appears that the recipients had close association with
the apostle.

"... the Spirit of the Lord will come upon thee, and you will be turned into another man."

—1 SAMUEL 10:6, NKJV,
THE NEW OPEN BIBLE

Chapter 13

The Anointing

As I've already stated, the anointing is the very presence, power and authority of God. Because of the anointing, miracles take place. It was God's anointing that parted the Red Sea. The very presence, power and authority of God by the Holy Ghost also has opened blind eyes, caused the deaf to hear, the lame to walk and the dead to be raised.

The anointing can come upon you, be with you and live within you. In the Old Testament, the anointing rested only upon kings, priests and prophets. But in the New Testament, and ever since, this anointing rests upon, and in, individual believers.

Scripture says in 1 John 2:27, "But the anointing which ye have received of him abideth in you..." When the anointing comes upon an individual it is strictly for God's service, to bring glory to Him.

In the Book of Judges we learn that after the death of Joshua, judges ruled the nation of Israel for about 300 years, until the united monarchy was established under King Saul. During those 300 years, about sixteen judges ruled Israel. Among them were Othniel, Gideon, Samson and Deborah.

According to Judges 3:9-10, "the children cried out to the Lord and the Lord raised up a deliverer for the children of Israel by the name of Othniel." It continues, "The Spirit of the Lord came upon Othniel to judge Israel." He went out to war and the Lord delivered Cushan-Rishathaim, king of Mesopotamia into Othniel's hands.

Later on, in Judges 6:34, it says, "The spirit of the Lord came upon Gideon." After Israel had been in captivity for 70 years, God gave them great victory over the Midianites.

Judges 14:6 then describes the Spirit of the Lord coming mightily upon Samson. Samson was anointed to deliver the Israelites, who had been in captivity for 40 years, out of the hands of the Philistines. In the natural, Samson was a small man, but when the anointing came upon him, he was very strong and very determined.

The anointing will change you into a different person. First Samuel 10:6 says that, "the Spirit of the Lord will come upon thee, and you will be turned into another man" (*man*, used here, means "all mankind," regardless of sex).

It is the anointing that gets the job done. Paul said in 2 Corinthians 3:5, "Not that we are sufficient of ourselves to think any things as of ourselves; but our sufficiency is of God." Paul realized that it was not of his own ability to achieve or accomplish any work in the ministry, but it was done only by the divine ability of God. It is God that distributes the anointing. Man appoints, but God anoints.

Another great judge who judged Israel was Deborah. She was a wife, a prophetess, a judge, a patriot and a warrior! The same anointing that rested upon Othniel, Gideon and Samson, to do great and exploitative works for God, also rested upon Deborah.

In Judges 4, Israel was again held in captivity for about twentysome years by the Canaanites. The children of Israel cried out once more for deliverance. So the Lord anointed Deborah.

In verse 8, Barak said to her, "If thou will go with me, then I will go; If thou will not go with me, then I will not go." Go with him where? To battle!

Deborah also prophesied that the Lord would sell the enemy into the hands of a woman. So it happened that a woman took the nail from a tent and hammered it into the temple of Sisera's head.

According to 2 Corinthians 10:4, people—both women and men—will fight battles. The thing to remember is that the weapons of our warfare are not carnal, but they are mighty through God to the pulling down of strongholds.

Paul said in Ephesians 6:12, "For we wrestle not against flesh and blood, but against principalities, against powers, against the ruler of the darkness of this world; against spiritual wickedness in high places."

The Bible gives powerful testimony on how God's anointing came upon Othniel, Gideon, Samson and Deborah to get their specific assignments done. Today, this anointing comes upon many of us, including women, when God calls us to get a job done.

There is an anointing that comes with every gift. There is an anointing to sing, usher, minister, and so on. There also is an anointing that comes with every five-fold gift. Ephesians 4:11 says, "And he himself gave some to be apostles, and some prophets, and some evangelists, and some pastors and teachers."

Here again, the word *some* refers to the fact that God did not call every believer to stand in the office of the fivefold ministry. However, every believer is called to salvation, but not to stand in the office of the five-fold ministry.

The Bible says in Matthew 22:14, "Many are called, but few are chosen." We are talking about the chosen one, the one God has called to stand in the office of the fivefold ministry.

There is an anointing to pastor, preach, teach, evangelize, and to be an apostle. Whatever office you may stand in, there is a specific anointing that will come upon you. If you are operating out of your calling, the anointing will not be there.

In the Old Testament many fell dead operating out of their calling. Remember, the anointing is within you, but it also will come upon you. The fivefold ministry gift was given to equip the saints for the work of the ministry, for the building up of the body of Christ that they might come to a position of strength and maturity.

God will use and is using women mightily to equip the saints to do a better work in the ministry and to bring them to a position of strength and maturity. Who is man to tell God whom to use? God says in His Word that He is the potter and we are the clay? Who is man (meaning people in general) to say that a woman can teach or preach, but cannot pastor? The Lord gave—not man. God uses whomever He wants to.

Romans 9:20-21 says, "Oh man, who are you to reply against God? Will the thing formed say to him who formed it, 'Why have you made me like this?' Does not the potter have power over the clay...?" If a woman or man is called to preach, then the preaching anointing will come upon them. If they are called to teach, then a teaching anointing will come upon them. The same applies to pastors, evangelists and apostles. That anointing will come upon them to stand in that office. Man has nothing to do with it. Remember, it is God who distributes His anointing.

Scripture also says in 1 John 2:27, "the anointing which you have received from God abides in you, and you need not that any one teach you; but the same one teacheth you of all things, and is truth, and is no lie, and even as it hath taught you, you shall abide in him."

Many people take this scripture out of context, implying that we need no man to teach us. Well, that is not what God is saying. God is saying that we will need no man to teach us any new doctrine.

Paul said in Galatians 1:8, "For even if we or an angel

from heaven preach any other gospel to you, let him be accursed." God will never contradict His Word.

If we did not need man to teach us, then God would not have given the fivefold ministry gifts—for pastors, preachers, teachers, evangelists, and apostles. According to Ephesians 4:12, "They are to equip the saints for the work of the ministry and to build up the body of Christ by teaching and preaching the word of God to them because only the word of God can build, exalt, and edify."

Once again, women are indeed mightily used to equip and build the body of Christ.

One other truth about the anointing is that the level or amount of anointing is up to the recipient. There are different measures of anointing that can be increased or decreased. It can be decreased by not spending enough time with God in prayer, reading or studying the Bible. If we spend sufficient, dedicated time alone with God in prayer and studying the Bible, the anointing will increase.

You do not get more of Jesus; Jesus wants to get more of you. As you yield, submit, and surrender to the Holy Ghost, it becomes less of you and more of God. John the Baptist said he must decrease and Jesus must increase.

"And so, after he had patiently endured, he obtained the promise."

—HEBREWS 6:15

Chapter 14

As a Pastor

I've already mentioned how even as a small child, I realized that I deeply wanted to one day become a teacher of the gospel. But I did not know I was going to be a pastor until 25 years later. Through the years my walk with God became so real to me, I could literally see Him.

You may ask how could that be. I could see Him through the eyes of faith. I would say to the Lord, "I can't see You with my natural eyes, but I can see you through faith." My faith had grown to be so strong, it was as if I could actually see Him as a physical man. I then began to experience many different oppositions in my life. I did not know that God was perfecting the ministry that was on the inside of me and was preparing me for a great work.

My brethren, ministry is just like pregnancy. I know about pregnancy, because of the birth of my beautiful children. Just as natural pregnancy, so it is with the spiritual birthing process. You have to carry that ministry and then give birth to it. God implants this seed in you, and it has to be carried until full maturity in order for it not to be premature and ineffective. Your ministry has to be carried, cared for, nourished and, finally, tested, before you actually give birth to it naturally. You first carry it spiritually, then in time you give birth to it; it will manifest in the natural. You learn as you go through tests, trials and tribulations. It allows a spiritual growth to take place.

The two most important things you learn to do is to stand and to remain faithful. Through experience you learn to be faithful to the Word of God and faithful to that which you confess and believe. God is spiritually making you and getting you ready for whatever is to be manifested in the natural.

The reason why many believers go through so much is because God's calling on their life is so great. The stronger your persecution, the stronger your anointing. It is going to take God's anointing to get the job done. God knows just how much anointing you need to complete your assignment. Therefore, go through what you have to go through.

Notice in Acts 14:22, Paul says, "Confirming the souls of the disciples, and exhorting them to continue in the faith, and that we must through much tribulation enter into the kingdom of God." Consequently, we see God is not setting you back in order to curse you. Rather, He is setting you up in order to bless you.

Trust the Holy Ghost. It will all work out for your good. Paul told Timothy, "God is only making first-class soldiers to take the frontline to lead others into the kingdom of God." (See 2 Timothy 2:1-5.)

Learn to pray something similar to this: "Lord, you don't have to make another (insert your name here). I will follow Paul's example. I will run my own race, fight my own fight and finish my own course. You don't have to raise up another me to finish what You called me to do. If anything, Lord, someone can simply pick up where I leave off when I die and go to be with You in heaven."

Jesus did not seek another to complete His mission or finish His course. He did it Himself with the power of the Holy Spirit. When the Holy Spirit came, He did not have to finish Jesus' work. He picked up where Jesus left off and He dwells in us and admonishes us.

Ministry has to be developed before it can be effective. An in-depth training process must take place. God first calls you, trains you, and then commissions you to go. A seed is planted and has to blossom to a full-grown fruit.

Peter said in 1 Peter 1:7, "That the trial of your faith, being much more precious than of gold that perisheth, though it be tried with fire, might be found unto praise and honour and glory at the appearing of Jesus Christ:" God will test your faith to see whether it is strong and pure.

Paul said in Galatians 5:22-23, "But the fruit of the Spirit is love, joy, peace, longsuffering, gentleness, goodness, faith, meekness, temperance: against such there is no law." These fruits of the Spirit have to be developed in your life in order for your ministry to be effective. It is very important that your faith and patience are perfected. If not, you will easily give up and become impatient and drop out of the race.

We are told in Hebrews 6:15, "And so, after he had patiently endured, he obtained the promise." Faith and patience will cause you to inherit the promise. Faith says, "It's done." Patience says, "I'll wait on it."

In Romans 5:3, Paul said, "to glory or rejoice in tribulations knowing that tribulations produce patience." God will allow trials and tribulations to produce and perfect our patience. In other words, God will allow your patience to be developed by you experiencing certain tests and trials because without patience you will not inherit the promise.

God has given you a vision for your ministry or calling. Without perfected faith and patience you will become impatient and give up. Being mature in your faith and patience, will enable you to stand firm until the manifestation of your vision comes to pass.

As you watch your ministry grow, be careful when you say, "We're going somewhere!" I went through a very sorrowful experience when God revealed His heart to me and how He feels when men and women in ministry say, "We're going somewhere."

Many who utter such statements may not realize that they are saying so under the influence of a demonic force called "deception." God told me that many of His people are deceived by the enemy, and are not aware of the trap of deception.

Many say, "I'm going somewhere," with visions and dreams of big church buildings, large congregations, fine homes and expensive cars. They speak these worldly things and are unaware that this could be self-exhortation and flesh glory. The Bible says pride comes before the fall.

There is nothing wrong with having big churches, fine homes and nice cars, but it has to be with the right motive. Many who speak these words are not aware that they are saying it out of the wrong spirit. If men and women of God are going to say, "We're going somewhere," let it be with the mind and the motive of adding souls to the kingdom of God!

As you preach the Word of God and as souls are added to the kingdom of God, and your ministry begins to increase, God will give you bigger churches and con-gregations, and if you desire, nice homes and cars.

Stop trying to duplicate other pastors and ministers— you should want to be original. God made you unique. You have a personality all your own. Why try to be someone else when God has anointed you to be that special and unique person?

There is an anointing upon you to reach a certain group of people in a certain way. If everybody had the same personality and style, then who would you reach? Be yourself—don't try to be somebody else.

Oftentimes the reason God cannot bless you the way He wants to is because you may be living a lie and a counterfeit life. That is not the real you if you are trying to be somebody else. If you want to be that person, then that person is going to receive your blessings because you want to be him or her and not yourself.

Why despise who you are? The way you walk is the way you walk. You are special to God! God has made you to be a certain unique person. If you want to be like someone else, then desire to be like the Christ that is in that person.

When Paul said, "Follow me as I follow Christ," he was speaking of being an example. Yes, we are to be examples. But the person you want to be like is Christ.

No two people are going to preach, sing or minister the same exact way. Aaron did not try to be Moses and Elisha did not try to be Elijah. You see, Elisha desired the power Elijah had, not his personality. Elisha did not say that he wanted to be like Elijah, as far as the way he walked and talked. No, instead, he wanted that power. As a matter of fact, he asked for a double portion. You desire to be all that God has called *you* to be.

Do not be a people-pleaser, instead be a God-pleaser. Don't you know that people-pleasers are miserable people? When you are a people-pleaser, you put your trust in others—not God. Proverbs 3:5 tells us to trust God with all our heart, and not man.

In addition, Jeremiah says in Jeremiah 17:5, 7, "Bless the man who puts his trust in the Lord, curse the man who puts his trust in another man." If you start your ministry off trusting in man, you will have to end up trusting in man. Remember, man will fail you.

Do not be a "respecter of persons" in ministry! Do not be afraid to rebuke, correct and chastise when needed. Be strong and courageous. Oftentimes I have observed pastors being too scared or intimidated to rebuke or correct certain members. Many times these were church members who were giving a lot of money to the church. So what? Their salvation is worth more than their money.

So what if the enemy says they might leave the church. So what if they do. Are you going to stop trusting God? God forbid! If you are afraid to speak the truth to them because they might leave, then guess what, your trust is really in man and not God.

If your trust is in man, then that means man has to bless you and not God. If you let God do it, He will use man to bless you. In Luke 6:38, God said, "I will use men to give into your bosom." But it will be God and His way, not yours.

So laugh at the devil and say, "Lucifer, you have lost again. One thing I recognize about you is that you are getting good at losing your cases! Keep losing, devil!" Remember, through all the bad, see the good.

Chapter 15

A Final Word

Throughout history, controversies have arisen concerning the proper role of women in the church. Women, as well as all believers, have been and always will be a very vital and integral part in spreading the gospel and furthering God's kingdom here on earth.

As you prayerfully study God's Word and spend quality time seeking His face, I am confident you will come to know your purpose. My prayer is that you learn the significance of walking by faith and not by sight. Receive everything from God first in the spirit by faith; then the Holy Ghost will manifest it in the natural.

I hope and pray that men and women will keep an open mind and heart concerning women who truly are called by God to be teachers, preachers, evangelists, pastors and apostles. After all, as the Bible says, God's Word *will* be preached.

Once you have been anointed, do not let anyone persuade you to believe that you have not received a divine calling, or that God cannot use you because of man's opinion. Know your purpose and know that the Holy Spirit dwells in you and He will direct you in fulfilling your mission.

As Proverbs 3:5-6 says, "Trust in the Lord with all thine heart; and lean not unto thine own understanding. In all thy ways acknowledge him, and he shall direct thy paths."